The Anonymous Bone

By

Donavon Davidson

For
Burlington, VT

Acknowledgements

It was 1998 and I walked to North Beach and took the trail to Lone Rock Point. I stood on the edge and looked out on the Adirondacks and felt the expanse within me. I wandered through Lakeview Cemetery with K. It was a cool and rainy October morning. We made our way to Kountry Kart and I had my first rise and shiner on the steps of City Hall overlooking the park. We drank wine in the afternoon and read Rimbaud. I spent hours sitting on benches on Church St. listening to musicians and children playing. The leaves of the honey locusts turned yellow then fell like confetti. I lived alone on Murray St., planted a garden, and fell in love with Lorca. Spent late evenings at Halversons listening to jazz. I worked mornings at Onion River Co-op and met the strange and beautiful artists and fellow lost souls. Then one day everything changed.

"Among a few dead cornstalks, the starving shadow of a crow leaps to his death."

from Sitting in a small screen-house on a summer morning

-James Wright

Contents

When I left for the world of empty bottles

When I left for the world of empty bottles,
the place where no ladders exist,
where boroughs swallow the moon
because they are tired of death,
the world of no dawn,
the invisible wounded world,
I gave my heart a beating.
My body became known to me
and I remembered the word useless.

Then a young girl cried
because a snowflake refused to melt.
I couldn't teach her how to smile
so I asked God to kill her.

I feel ashamed to tell you why. But
stay with me. Make me forget awhile.
I still remember how my leg fell to pieces
and how I complained like a waterfall
or a sudden departure of birds.

Make me forget about that field
too concerned with the utter ruin of a habitat,
where I would like to go.

I still remember
the slow motion of a fist
swinging through the air
with its invisible heart.

There is an unknown child waiting for me

There is an unknown child waiting for me
where the moon has ripped her clothes
exposing milk and wax.

I could not resist her.
As the nocturnal flower opened
I dreamed a cloud had cut her throat
and wept in the twilight of murder.

When the mourning doves saw what was done
they removed their veils,
letting me alone carry their snow.
It was their only way of protecting me
from the carriage of violet light
where baskets of butterflies
leave their prints cold as nails
behind the wrists of headless Madonnas.

Someone is sleeping next to me,
hiding in the shadows of my curtains.
Someone who no longer needs to sleep
has worked a vast nation of flurries
reoccurring through a dream of winter caskets,
sealing my lips with wax.

Searching the Cancellations

You made eyes with me
to adore the inverted night
impersonating insomnia.

All the fleet animals of its derelict wind
intently gazed upon
whatever nativity of tears
you let form into glass bells
withholding preserved footprints,
and it was enough to keep them
sleeping in an orchard
trussed to the sound of dropping fruit,
by whose drab beauty
translated into exhaustion.

The somber rains left lewd imprisonments
harkening the clatter of coins
in a blind man's cup.
Confessions sought in the throats of wolves,
never in the bones draped
in the loosely fitting coats of beggars.

I thought of all the streets,
their abandonment of history,
but not their treatments of unanswered excellence.
I thought of the museums
of impressionistic returns,
their walls ladened with secret touches.

They gave us the glinted ghosts
that never stopped trying to consecrate
the hole from which, any minute,
we throw ourselves forward
 into a gallop of disclosures.

My living goes on and on
being punished by contemplating cancellations,
while you cannot recall one fire
not starting from another.

When you made the green leaf red
I could not stop pursuing the invisible force
that shook it to the ground.

One day I will untangle the tender shadow
of a scar most birds understand
as a place where dreams are left
to open their pink mouths.

And you will tell me to look
upon the nervous scratching of this century
and find a God small enough to swallow
or starve.

Should ladders hang alone in trees

Should ladders hang alone in trees
and the sad forgotten hallways
fasten your heart with a dead hand,
rub the wounds of exile from your neck
and strike the pure jaw of vanity.

Lips that no longer open
imitate the sounds of farewell,
and what you've killed is jealous of your living.
They want to bring you back
in bottles of wine and poisoned livers,
intent on drowning your lungs
with the smoke of your burning.
These tenuous spirits of fear
are praying to Judas for hope.

It is not a dream that shadows come to life
oily from the birth of curtains.
And it is not by chance they are young,
holding mirrors for eyes,
fighting your doubt with doubt.
It is your life to re-live that sends you running
eager for the lamb of courage.
You are the father of knives!

Because you know you must hang
to untie yourself,
you turn away the children who have no eyes.
Because you know you must strike

the tread of innocent ballots
where the academies of prudence
dissect the rent space of blood,
there is a book that goes unwritten
and you see yourself as something.

Push on you tendril orchard of flesh

Push on you tendril orchard of flesh.
Heaven's machine is in her swirling ankle
belling mad. Yet, in my animal atom,
Alpha Zero, the sound is heard wolfed.

Love is a horn that fitfully blows
all the long-tongued shadows
blasting from her breast, peeling my skin
like shingles from a dry thatch.

The flickering swath of craving. That muscling bow
swinging from love's hook. Deaf and singing dumb,
I was blinded by her birthing sun upon snow
grand zeniths. Air like needles in my lung.

So, bidding farewell to the distant crying bellows
for her blithe song, abandoning my drum
and my wounded heel to the wind,
I rode high the pale ark to its zero.

Push on you strange marvel that axes my cleft,
the broad lusting thermals of my meridian.
No more shall you stir my alien anthology
or lower my outright vitals to your curves.

Pull out your novel unheeded infant
who hunts in the south, injuring my left thigh.
No more shall there be a wounding of the bright
arcadian wax in the ankle belling zero-hour.

So, Farewell you long-tongued phantoms licking
an ivory blade, the cipher of her rib.
Curling in the crush of her heaving
apple, cooling my cherished Adam.

Put away the rumor of my past ruin
and fingering lust in your true-tongued mirror.
Your dim organ blows me from the crown of Canaan,
riding high the pale ark to its zero.

The good shopkeeper cursed the morning

The good shopkeeper cursed the morning
for his dead leg was a purple ribbon.
The cunning moneylenders locked their doors
and the brute trade said a prayer
for the casual traffic of ramparts.

The locusts suddenly let their hair down
in a parade of glittering gold
blinding empty sleeves of their toy guns,
gathering excitement in crippled laps.
For the echoing horns of gunfire
have robbed the dead.

The velvet dress of a young woman
the color of a dark plum or burgundy
was blushing as she spilled by
ruining the hearts of benches,
transfiguring a host of ambush.

As the good shopkeeper fell into his rank,
a factory of metal rubbed his heal
while bankers hid in their walls
                rubbed with chalk.

A single candle in a window
dimly shook the darkened trench.
And as the wind blew a flush of velvet,
the heart of the night
played its drum of phantoms.

An old woman fell on the sidewalk

An old woman fell on the sidewalk
watched by the plastic fashions.
The sleeping lights in the trees
              were still unborn.

While behind the glass,
the barren models had no hands.
No one saw her gown of chains
shatter into a flight of pigeons.
For, the children were being led away.

Unknown men were dressing
lampposts with garlands of freshly cut fir.
Tiny fingers of juniper
            could be heard dripping
while the cracked bed of excrement crystallized
below the bodiless limbs.

No one remembered their names
or why they amputate for steel.
For, the children were being led away.

They have taken the clock from the tower
so their hands may be endlessly stacked.
There is a signaling model of stillborns
           in luxurious colors.
Sometimes old women fall on sidewalks
watched by the plastic ton.

Suddenly your hair was

Suddenly your hair was
the street of fallen women

disfigured by pulsing neon,
unsexing vacant stairs,

extinguishing beds to oblivion,
luring imaginations
into trembling scenes of smoke.

The lurid kiss of strangers
swaddled like a Christ
in freshly soiled straw.

Hiding thumbs behind your neck,
the bleating wool hung
dryer than caked blood
from the lips of raped whores.

Suddenly,
no one was aware
and my eyes lowered
unable to hold your shame
of terrible redemption.

Your bodice of hair
opened its room of candles
with infinite labors of crosses.

Your shroud of arbors,
a trembling profile of neon,
wept in a violent smoke.

Mother of children

Mother of children
will you have me again?
I crave the danger of lead
and the sweet poison of ash.
You came to me in a dream
defiant as the moon.
As I wept you filled yourself
finer than grains of salt
and the nocturnal aloes
bled through my wounds.

Your love has sent me running.
Entering the home of cowards
I threw myself against the clay
in a childish tantrum
and filled my absence with sterile wine
betraying our tapers of advent.
The endless nights of angels
forgot their wings of bloody urine.
I had no way of harboring
such a reckless courage,
so I took to strange beds of wondering
until the devils of sobriety appeared.

Such awakenings of hands!
That page of blank purity
was spinning its wheel
birthing lambs of pica,

bearing sparrows in a tea cup,
feeding me earth
and the fragile sky.

Reading Adam

Don't believe every tragedy has been written.
We do not have to gather our tears
and nail them to each green tip of spring
in hopes God will speak to us.

Just wait until I turn the lights off.
You can run your fingers through my hair.
You can walk on broken glass
if you let your eyes adjust to the light.

I promise you the one animal
I could never name
will show you the body
that denies survival
is the body that refuses desire.

Tell me, what do you see?
I am not allowed to follow,
for he who has no name
in the mirror
has drowned me in myself,
has left only eye lashes of a baby,
a barb-wire fence dividing two fields of snow.

I would tell you the only tracks to follow
are the drops of blood, to have faith
they lead back to your own hands,
but you are searching my mouth
for a lover who died of exposure

by trying to rescue a child in a house of chamber music
set ablaze by his father
who fell asleep smoldering.

You say each tooth is now just a gravestone
with no name, a grace note that must be felt
and not counted.

Love letters returned unopened

My failure in knowing the difference, you said,
was knowing the difference

of the jawbone of a man
from the killing of your boy.

Ghosts who do not know they're dead,
merely lighting one candle with another
feel my shouldering into a new world,
an atlas of passage to a faster sun rise.

A woman who reddens a statue's lips
because she cannot speak her own prayers,
who returns every morning
with fruit that must rot
for her prayers to be answered,
spills milk upon my shoulders
to prove she is no different.

Our ritual of undressing leaves us with nothing more
than to search for someone we don't know.

Of course you know the best place
to find a hole you cannot fall into
is in my ribs.

To close my eyes and say, guess who is here
and who thinks they can name the song,
not of the caged bird, but the one who thinks
it is free to come and go.

I know you want me to believe it's you
not me, but I can only open one eye.
The other remains closed, a blind spot
where I must turn my head to look behind me,
to avoid collision.

Consider the meteor
hurtling from the hands of our dark lord.
The impression we're left with is nothing
more than a reflecting pool
from which we gaze into the image of light
without looking up.

Here I confess Hiroshima was nothing new.
It had little to do with staying up past midnight
and everything to do with watching the sun set
for the first time.

Do not believe every bed becomes a wonderland
of impossible rides.
Here we hold on for dear life.

I will forever see the corners

I will forever see the corners
that are vacant from your crush
of little feet that mob your lips.

Many times your push of hair
held its secret of surrender
beyond my hope of deluge.

In your sensitive prison of nipples
you refuse my lock of kisses,
possessing my mouth to submission.

I tried to overthrow your absence
with vain idols still un-skinned
and defile your empty bed.

But, they too ran pale of magik
and left a trail of lime
that always led back to you.

So many walls I have built
around the beds of skeletons
while their hearts fall to pieces!

Opening your blouse of coronas,
I am reminded of our estrangement
in the easy kicking of virgins.

The lake could be a robe of fire

The lake could be a robe of fire.
The moon could be a house of wealth.
The child who flashed her smile
        could be a sickle of plagues.
The towering cloud has a promise of bleach,
a cypher in its egg of cancer.
A woman passed by whispering this
while her corpse hung from her scarf.

I believed for a long time that my father's ghost
could not lie so beautifully as my shadow.
I would stain my skin with fragrant offerings
        and refrain from obvious mirrors.
A plume of crabs scuttled from his pipe
cascading down wooden albas
insinuating the night of dissolving profiles.
And I remember the corner of webbed arrows
        and taste their stiff dust.
Having no longer a need for hunting
I lay with my cancer in a naked quiver.

His name was a dagger of silence.
His leather was the devil's trill.
His eye for me swallowed whole
        every candle of birth.
Indeed, the lake could be a robe of fire
for I no longer believe I am absent
        in shadow or reflection.

Believing in Me

Pen and paper,
you have failed to prove I exist.

You appear as nothing more
than a ball of darkness
that has unraveled, silk
that spiders weave into veils.

Mirrors,
I suspect you know something I don't.
Saying I have passed this way
sometimes naked, sometimes
dressed to kill.
Along with the straight razor
and the butcher's knife,
you thought I'd be the one
to slit my own throat.

I have only to close my eyes
and listen for the places
light will never visit.
Where mice chew holes in churches
just the same as in coffins.

There, it is still possible to hear
a small boy whistling in a dark alley
of a dream.
He tells me it is only a bird
singing in its own egg.

Autumn leaves are falling.
They are our only way of seeing.

He places them on the ground,
leaving them to be buried
in the reds of their rustling.

So that when a strong wind blows,
I can hear where they're coming from.

It isn't enough

It isn't enough
to silence the hands of an hour.
It isn't enough
to remember the sound of a word.
It isn't enough
to visit the blood of empty hands.
This sky withheld its Saturn
but would not refuse its burden.
Then the street closed its eyes
and a murder went unnoticed.

There will be nights of sad journeys
with impossible bells of the dead,
and days of such frenetic bondage
that only children dare ask why.
But it will not cool the urge to poison
because it is not enough.
It is not enough
to remove our clothes as if we cared
if the skin of suicide tightened like a drum,
and, if with one last look
we cried because we were happy,
happy because we knew
that it wasn't enough
to consume the sighs of skeletons.

All my twisted sleepers are ramming steel

All my twisted sleepers are ramming steel.
All my past leaders are heaving silent.
And, as my safety goes crashing in my wielding,
my lasting goes loudly as they watch.
It's time to let the flowers grind.
It's time for surrender like watching blooms.

Ice can break at night.
Still, eyes are blind.
Ice can break at night
like heroes dying from their wounds.

All my perennial fears are jamming sunflowers.
All my tender horrors are but tickling sins.
And, as my green vapor goes wafting from my wing,
my blazing goes splitting in my wind.
It's time for level courage: from pollen to germ.
The time has come, the freezings wake.

Ice can break at night
like secrets unlearned.
Ice can break at night
when the uncoiling wakes.

My heartbeat rocks the bed

My heartbeat rocks the bed.
The hammering recoil, pulse, and spring
sent the waking flocks, bleeding
stigmatas of my soil, bereft of slumber.

My coiling vein undoes its jaw.
The hunger now thick within its chambers
sent a sweet blue pain of Job
sleeping in the milk sick swallowing clasp.

My burden rests in that murmur.
The quick eye of that dream gives air
sent rising from my chest rushing to my mouth
sounding like downy beams of tender acts.

My refluxing space is filled with visions.
The horrible capture forced to flame
sent rapid tremors to pace its volumes
succumbing to a brilliant luster of passion's flower.

Let me burn or drown in my sickle gene

Let me burn or drown in my sickle gene.
The very cell that breaths ore,
is doubled on the wicked
anvil, is flush with the love
of a terrible home.
Why do all the cells flail
across this flood, and chains,
would as I were, stretch
the fixed flames of dust?
To all a great vine leaving a slick
I could extend with mettle,
if I were too wise.

Let it come the great sex of the sun.
But, that I may have vision.
For every atom making
womb after womb, jam
a sea in my virgin gravity.
Why do I go blind in the heat
of dropping blood and swallow
the innocent seeds,
would as I were, eager
in the lot where April's flares
yield the horns of fall?
The drifting land grows weak from the sea
I could bray and bell,
if I were much too wise.

So I'll burn in this hour's day.
A star in iron ore,
a pure jewel in coal,
folds me in its waters
punishing the vapid edges.
Why does the giant dome plunge
its windy tides and stroking
the cellular bellows,
would as I were, quickening
the carbon plot black for babes?
It glows like a moon on a nail
I would curse and yield with balance,
if I were wise to its very angle.

My country and the thin communion

My country and the thin communion
because bruised petals of the drooping
charm, this alabaster claw hanging
across my cage. As if these hooking
strings could whisk my lamping ton,
my country. And the thin communion,
harboring the ruddy speedy drug
in silent narrows of a greeting,
never lets my boarders quick to run.

My limbus in the dog jowl fold
because I hoard the four pentacles
against my hip, my awkward fertile
axing sod. As if these graves mingle
in a strange mass to lay down my soul,
my limbus. In the dog jowl fold
all pure milestones in the quick mud,
lifeless lambs heaped in a butchers pile,
groan in the full verge hushed in their roll.

My Sodom pushing the gallant blow
because the sensual bounty wanes
in anguish, the shock of exchange
with barren hope. So I lift my lame
channel and suffer in my hell throws,
my Sodom. Pushing the gallant blow
I rest easy in my plot of blood,
my country. Where all the cells remain
greater than all the love that I show.

And if I said to you

And if I said to you
that hope never spoke to me
while in the fields green
nave and cannon

although I leapt like lightning
through rows of August
silk and flesh-

That hope was silent in
a pitiful country heaping
limbs to boarders

although I swam wide
through the howling wisps of
root and strata-

That hope was unforgiving
and shed its weight upon
back and breast

although I was but a child I
threw my frame and hued the
breadth and distance-

And if I said to you
that hope no longer shrinks
leaving a hollow cast
lead and clay

that hope, like folly,
waits in my vision
dark and feminine.

Although I do not know where it comes from
I see her, now, as it should be.

Hope is a tender prism.
How delicately it blends
milk and blade.

The nights have cast a pledge

The nights have cast
a pledge,
a fitful longing
to grow old on such things.

They have bore us out
righteous gallows,
no sleeve on this place
to bewilder the heathers,

though it's gently calling
like a jingle shell bodice,
its hunger digs
through our nebula -

An open fist shaking
the hounds at bay to
a thundering echo that tremors
the quintile heavens.

Slowly, as if by the ring waves
of a tree,
we feel the subtle
skin of birth.

Slowly, the quivering animal
in my bone
ascends to its call

and
lay down.

There is no way out of this thing.
We have done ourselves in!

When I rose

When I rose then from my bed, I moved
rivers inside a sand grain
and let them drift into a scrub brush
drifting into a dune.

When I woke the millionth sun cooling
in the dropped off rain,
I let them set on petals
and, I let them set in the bloom.

When I took my first breath, I was given
everything the heavens had to give.
Sending it quickly back again.
Taking it quickly back again.

When I moved, I sent tremors
through the terrible winds humming.
My fist dug through the currents lash,
yet I let this front remain.

When I spoke, characters, impossible
language, leapt like tigers running,
and then tearing outward as to eat them,
and then tearing inward just the same.

And, when I thought of this, my heart
leapt and left me.
Rising…

Drifting…
A million suns!
A drop of heaven!
Sent through this swart geometry.

Examining the Ashes

All I wanted to know was why
that thing over my shoulder
was raving like a lunatic.
Why things on paper
have fields of light
by means of finger movements.

There! That spot on my back.
That stain that shadow
that random cry heard at night.

What can studying its star of nativity
tell you about this wax
dripping in a basin of water?
What patterns of becoming dizzy and falling down
can accidentally be seen?

Had it been a woman holding a fountain
or a child bearing a passage of smoke
I would have gladly taken a second look.
For looks can be deceiving
and all these blind people
leading all these blind people
is how we got this far in the first place
and that we can't tell
what thing behind us
if it's scratching in the ash
or is set to crow at daybreak

or if its sacrificed laughter
such as all the sharp objects of sleep
foolishly parades around
as dust or old shoes.

Ode to Autumn

Today I felt her breast
as if a child yawned.
An incredible horizon
lying upon me.

I am not now resisting her breath…

How do I greet the giant in her rise?

How do I greet the giant in her rise?
No lamp or reason can brighten my aim,
arms length to an ocean of sun.
Its single shadow casts a swath of rage
sending me mad. Keeping me still.

How do I hold the giant in her eyes?
No hero or spirit can send me sane
along the atom of my rib where flesh runs
it's faint flicker of fragrance blasting the cage.
Sending me mad. Keeping me still.

And, how do I sooth the giant in her cry?
No cradle or tomb can ease this pain.
No prayer can wreck what's undone.
Its meaning falls deaf upon her page.
Sending me mad. Keeping me still.

How, tell me how to know this giant of lives?
When no wood or stone can keep its vein
and no question can reckon the answer's sum.
It's a wicked time and a curse of Age.
Sending me mad. Yet, keeping me still.

Wrap me in your bed clothes

Wrap me in your bed clothes.
It's in my nature to talk things to death.
It's in my nature to love things to death.
And if you say, "it is not in mine," then
wrap me in your bed clothes
for if these are not in yours, then
to hold you is well enough.

To trace the brow of your sleep
        down the pale nape that so
easily becomes your urging breast,
        urging me downwards
to the heavenly spiral, invisibly inward
        and rare to my touch.
The touch of my blood stained finger
trembles with oils from such a
fragrant plum and blushing,
from such a tottering overlay of essence.

Oh, very well then, this will have to do.

Once, when I was young

Once, when I was young,
I fell into a sea
and was happy not to find
the edges. But, my
lungs capped the waves
when the windy mountain
bent her knees.
And, so heavy was
her invasion, that not
a single nerve was
left unfeathered
as her death
fell
like a snowflake.

Down the street's festival

Down the street's festival,
below the brave moirés
crashing their furtive rainbows
spilling fragrant blinding aloes
on the yawn of iron archways
wherc spiders heave their anvils,
        death was shaking its windows
        as the children ran to play.

Among the calamities of brick,
basket weavers are working strings
with visible flesh stirring like hives.
They strum barren reeds alive.
Unclothing auroras of web and sling
where black legs signal it's quick,
        death was pushing its thighs
        as a bride took her ring.

Through the relentless mouthing fold,
bruised wine was subduing bells,
coarsely killing by inches
the crow of man to itch
the narrow liver's jade veil.
Where black silk cradles its crucibles,
        death was quivering its pitch
        as the drunk light was felled.

Suggestive lamps finger sworn beds
as the eventide speeds

the goatish seeds of nightshade
within an inch of being saved
from the harbor of bent knee.
Where sleeping spiders wait in webs,
    death was whipping the glass egg
    as a cradle cherished its wreath.

My muscle leans upon your vein.

My muscle leans upon your vein.
Pushing forward – pushing upward.
The scent of chemicals spiral upon
contact like wood from a plane.

Oh, how it begins: pale & pure.
So solemn is a craft of solitude
where the innocent visions of shapes
soon bleed and labor pitches lures.

It is not enough that you lunge
from your cell. But that my tools,
the rib and jaw, may plum the toil
of flesh on flesh in their graceful plunge.

Our muscles lean with veins.
pushing forward— pushing upwards.
One above, the other under.
Side by side, in motion the same.

You will lay thin as sheets
as I feel your folds and narrows,
your sleeping grain, yet never
leave a mark where we meet.

Steady on the carpenter's mean.
Not lifting ladders too soon
from these bodies' elements, swirling

metals. How they use caution as they teem.
                  Like giants of the dust-

The giants of the dust are talking,
who fell from your thighs like milk,
who embraced your globes and milled
the ancient tree that went rocking
Falling
by. Like
the stockings
at your feet.

All my tides in the world

All my tides in the world,
just a star in the
triangle of dust.
An ocean that once was, was
once an astral geometry
in the solar wind
of the lightsome god
who with ray flower in eye
and prophetic release
let that five arrows
gild one divine string.
So, like a newborn star,
I was aimless in my birth
and let my stellars
where they willed.

One fell on the tongues
of angels who, with beautiful
tendrils nurturing, taught me
Heaven's breast, and her infinite lap.
One fell on the fingers
of women who, with naked
flexing, fed me earth
between their thighs,
her eggshell arbor of fishes.
So pitiful in the world then fell
three needles blind, wriggling like
worms in their angle of dust,
Ishmael in their spleens.

Oh, what god or devil
now bends their rays!

And it was there, there
in the triangle of dust
the five teeming tides
became five echoes. And,
I won't say I was brave
when I saw the godly bow
lay like an amorous beach.
Its galaxy of shells,
once life's arrows,
now barren fossils,
made me shudder to see
their scattered clothes
that mapped the needle of flesh,
shrouding the naked geometry
where a light made its way.

I Come Out Wherever You Are

I counted and I counted
a hundred times the day
flew from one tree to another
and pecked at a litany of wild flowerings.

It was your idea
that its blue sky should never move,
that only storms come and go.

That I would be forgiven, too,
for having no end in sight.

But about this night, angel.
Is that my bright idea
I might have had going dim?

All I hear are shadows milling about,
grinding bones in their rusty mouths,
and I mistake a child hiding
beneath a sheet as a ghost.

All those disembodied voices
that jerk me out of sleep must be
your way of keeping me safe, angel.

Is that why you never answer
when I ask, who's there?

When you speak sometimes your words disappear

When you speak sometimes your words disappear,
tired of being words and tired words.
Knowing how tiny birds fly, they undressed.
But you leave me as if I startled you.
And I, too ashamed of my body, can't
follow. I am left suddenly alone
with this sad heaviness of your perfume
re-living our violence on my sleeve.

To feel you, I wore the face of a house
and the restless arms of forgiveness.
Left to no one but you to occupy,
I gave room after room of embracings.
Each with its terrible letting go.
I must have been easy to over run.
Not because I knew and let it happen,
but because I feared it would, then it would.

Now everything I own hides your body.
Even my own hands protest from your smell
so that everything I touch, now you touch.
Pursuing even my dreams with a look,
reassuring my heart with casualties
like, "this blade is for saving *and* killing."
I will no longer live within vague laps
where there is no murder just for caring.

So, if from your cradle of living beds
you hear me speak through the cover of dust,
knowing that every cruel act lies
bare, release that tiny bird from your throat.
Its young voice lifting a veil of ash
ready for the threshold of my scorched hair.
Not because I live in circles of smoke,
but because I do not pretend to know.

As the dark eye of something wild sees

As the dark eye of something wild sees,
as the trembling trees of a million blooms
keeps smiles through the love of insects,
we sleep in jealous rooms of open hands,
while cities of America collide.

Where subtle galleries were once silent,
where ideas of easy pollution
were conceiving the amateur marquis,
a shameless force swept like a stupid fire.
A gift for the children, we let it go.

Local idols never heard of sprang up.
releasing their hearts of burning vomit,
clothing the multitudes with a strange air,
dreaming of every possible war.
The envious room of hands moved like worms.

For every imaginable scream,
for every imaginable ghost,
unmentionable mercies became law.
Draped by the hide of ethnic purity,
statues of forgotten heroes went blind.

For those who believe they hear violins
among the awesome choir of lilacs
and the hypnotic drum in matted hair,
those who steal a kiss from the willing
are mirrors of skin still perfumed with blood.

In their ruinous waking of spent faith,
they no longer deny they're sabotaged.
Wearing the mask of an opening leaf,
putting words on their tongues like black crosses,
they arrange their banquette of skeletons.

While America sings the beautiful,
families of the dead horse plant lilies
in a carriage of disheveled mantels,
mixing wine with the ashes of their dead,
rehearsing the new fist of infamies.

As the cruel document of gay nails
hammers away their songs of vogue freedoms,
the capital sins of territory,
peopled with the dogs of oblivion,
starve innocent occupations of blame.

As the dreaming collective plays it's mass,
the untamed wildly yawn their slogan.
We are the lamp of the terrible fist;
we are the lamp of the terrible fist,
remembering the sun could never blind.

When morning comes some will forget the dreams,
the horrible dog killing dreams of thieves,
and stare through their working like a dumb saint,
(as the dark eye of something wild sees)
and sing - *America! America!*

What patience of unknown buildings

What patience of unknown buildings
blows hell from boarders of pleasure
bed to every bed this hour's
comedy when the coma rails.

Tabloid flesh of locomotives.
This is the tender joke, mother.
Empty threats for some pilgrimage,
metropolis of swallowed tongues.

There is a zero in our eyes.
And for this we thought we were wrong
to have our funeral lips
wake in dreams of new messiahs.

The sleeping steel never told
what towering spiders of smoke
remembered that day of flying.
To cradle the space of rent angels!

From here we cannot disturb them
with our cast of plastic acting
so we fear the pull of curtains.
Oh, mother, we need miracles!

Should our theatre of flesh cool
and the steel word strip us of fame,
while we wait for the shows wide lay,
to know why the curtain never
                    rises.

Inheriting the Earth

Better that I'm poor when I carry the egg
in the daylight. So sayeth the spoon
sleep blind from filling holes full of daydreamers.

The knife skulks in its glittering alter
to turn blood into butter and spread it thick
and you only live once and the stains
never come out.

The fork makes a bed of nails
to make the tongue go bye bye
which happens when the body's prone
sleeping in a room so close to the dead
which isn't a word for pain you've grown up with
but the one you've grown accustomed to.

And that, my child, is how the poor inherit the earth.

They balance eggs on their little spoons
and race towards the next gravedigger
who's been admiring their cherubim face in its mirror.

There are things more lonesome when you are near

There are things more lonesome when you are near.
There are thirty names that confuse my lips.
As I pronounce your note a stranger sighs,
lays about your nude, threatens your torso.
Imagine my sadness as I see him,
what I must witness again and again.
I must believe you are original.
Primitive faith, I shall embrace a god!

There is a breathless needle in my side
when sometimes your heat like wind vanishes,
sweeps clean your lap and the rub of that brute,
scattering pages down vacant alleys:
our novel mark void of that dead letter.
Let me close my eyes with this thought of you:
alone in your world, virgin latitude,
a rogue of protest and of sacrifice.

And when visions come, I will refuse them
and treat them as though they were a thief.
Divine horrors they have laid about you,
hallucinations of pure surrender,
where even God may lay with you awhile.
Fearful of the child they one day might steal,
I fill the valleys where your heart has cleaved,
like it was my grave or the cup of Christ.

Now this, a silent moment of crossing

Now this, a silent moment of crossing,
known only to the hands worked with gold,
see the hour of bridges as a veil.
The histories of paper left to their backs
(See how tiny their careful steps marked)
tangle in the rushes of cut flowers
until they are themselves a fading perfume
hung from a wall or between pages -
their meaning hushed in the hearts of candles.
Nothing remains in the kiss of passing,
the intimate space of a flame, nothing.

And now, may the country of our hands open
and people themselves across your body.
Towering cities bursting in your touch,
inventions of wild blood in your lock
refuse the push of ice upon your age.
Dashing within the borders of your nave
together no more homeless than the wind,
more innocent than the labor of stars,
you escape the very meaning of love.

Let these words you hear undress themselves
so that there is nothing left between us.
That quiet distance between our bodies
is a horizon that has no language.
Elusive as the service of twilight,
glimmering candles or constellations,
nothing can occupy your pure embrace.

Enemy of sun, you are brighter,
burning away paper statues of words
that can neither bond nor call you by name.

Bring me distance or rooms of liberty

Bring me distance or rooms of liberty
for these are vacant days
that measure this and measure this.
Do not come for my beauty
with your letch full of crosses,
wild flower, and a shudder of stars.
In-between the rooms there is no name.
Ah, but when I look at you all at once,
when I look at you
between the rooms…

Before you burn the casual event,
before you sound a broken frame,
(what could be the laughter of our child)
humming in the very place you don't want,
(and that long day of drunk heaven
sent word to the shuddered and the damned
blackening with the very weight of our tiny embers),
remember that there are other rooms
waiting for you.
There are so many.
May this one have the strength to send you back to God.
Let this one be enough.

Whatever will town the gentle tables of your time,
whatever choice you burn to light your way,
during your season of apples
when moonflowers surrender to the night
signaling to dream the perfume of forgetful prints,

there will always be the rumor of heavy wines
filling your glass with a devils tattoo.
Always and always
so whatever.

If you should find me as a vacant hour
do not come for my beauty.
When I am a casual moment
I should think that I am truly free.
And I am dreaming that you are not a book.
Then your un-opening beauty
hangs in the airs wild calamity,
its desolation corrupt with suggestive regards,
and a hollow in your curves goes undamaged.

But when I look at you all at once
I see the casualties in your curves
beautifully twisting a millions fires
that burn me into simple embers.
So I cool, so I cool,
in the passing of my freedom
from the handsome parlors of jezebels
somewhere in-between your casualties of beauty.

Tears hang upside down to me

I might have listened when I wrote this
and forgave myself once and for all.
I might have laughed at myself, laughing
as I tricked the Holy Ghost
with its cure eating my own kiss.
It has never been so easy
to have told a tear strung with a lie,
blushing with naves, it has never been.

For years I was a country of boys
who were young in laps of the world.
For years the love of mother's loving
would only wash away tears.
And we saw their hands as cruel joys
waving goodbye, we thought, as we played
letting go in an exile of arms.
Home fell down my cheek waving goodbye.

So I drag and inch into a thaw.
Which is the cool treasure of my worm.
So I cannot cheer my nerves, cheering
with the quick range of rumors
only stills my mouth with a fools haul.
What I have done to my breast remains
lodged as rings in a tree, waiting the
fearful cutting of what I have done.

This is the trouble of what I know.
Can you tell I am a lost city?

This is my smile of graves, smiling
cadavers who beat and chime
with their curses pretty as your toes.
If I could forget how the dead lie
and forgive myself once and for all
I could be yours, if I could forget.

Has it been too much my crowd of hearts?
I see you are a babe in my hand.
Has it been the end of me, ending
in all the loving mothers
calling me home with their tear strung harps?
I have never been a good morning
until your smile scissored those tears.
Until today, I have never been.

Love Only Happens in the Rain

You are and the empty chair,
two wine glasses ringing out
over a city asleep,
a wooden box filled with hand-me-downs
making something out of nothing to fear.

You are
and a birdhouse under a fern
adopts the dust
and the one under our bed,
shadows cast in our minds
and the one in the basement
collects the drips
where the heart leaks -

a thing with wings,
one red leaf,
a snowflake.

Love only happens in the rain,
nothing to run our fingers through
what fell and fell.

The world won't hate a thing
that drops clean out of the blue
and you are and you have been.

Tell me again and again
rather definitively
these flowers cannot run away.

Under the Rose

When I left you in the morning
I wanted to beg forgiveness.

I wanted to buy for you
all the valleys of yellow.

The day your heart stopped speaking
through the scent of my fingers

I have tried to be a thief
and creep through your sleeping hair.

Maybe the wind was careless,
as I have been when I laughed,

overlooking something there,
something too small to cry out.

But the night was starving too,
more lonesome than my caged mouth,

and I couldn't tell you how
it reminds me of your breast.

Because I am just a man
who found forgiveness in dreams,

but forgot what it was like
to see a butterfly's nude

or say the word yellow.
Though your body holds much more

will you be just a woman?
Waiting for no one to say

any more than you let them,
let yourself be beautiful.

Even though I can't tell you
still I wish, under the rose.

So be them unlike the weight of six feet

So be them unlike the weight of six feet.
When heaven kisses the skin with its screws,
let the damn frost cool lips that do not speak.

Whosoever wishes the tongues of sleep
dumb as hooves save for those cattling crews,
so be them unlike the weight of six feet.

When those lunged miracles blow the lamb's teeth
rank with angeled mothers barren with news,
let the damn frost cool lips that do not speak.

High in their drugged hair they strangle the creeps,
fucked in their locks, mad as vanity's nude.
So be them unlike the weight of six feet.

Happy as sweethearts who will never meet
clowns with kisses, till the earth fills their shoes,
let the damn frost cool lips that do not speak.

So I wish, should I break on lovers' knees.
Hell is for the wrecked throws that linger, too,
so be them unlike the weight of six feet,
let the damn frost cool lips that do not speak.

Where the great escape of your spinning wheel

Where the great escape of your spinning wheel
gave away your hour of sleeping hips,
home of the innocent ovens angeled
with the shape of tears from clouds of cancer,
things you have seen signing away with the
language once and for all smells of childhood,
your hands became a dreamer once again.

This is the earth that must carry a cup.
It must be very empty for spilling.
It came from the sky, the sky where nothing
lives in peace, for there is no sleeping there.
And you have shown the bed between your hands.
And you have gathered the eyes of fences,
and you have remembered to set them free.

This is the sea that I have never known.
What lives in the lungs of water, always
leaving, always coming back again, so
I cannot hold my breath for very long.
And it isn't a way of holding on
and being shaped by where I cannot be
and waiting for what I have never known.

Every wave is a wheel giving away
its breaking hip to be held by a hand.
This is the freedom I have never choose,
nor would I, having known it could have been

the difference between a rising statue,
dark leviathan of smoke in the sky,
awake! Or, the dreaming cup of your hands.

Snow Globes

Thieves from the land of cotton were led away quietly.
The man hunt of the century was finally put to bed.
This after a bear was lynched
and a horse split open
like a bloody pillow.

The sight of all these stuffed animals
demanding retribution
was a thing of beauty.
For I could see something swirling
behind their glass eyes
and I knew I was something
that could be shaken
and not blow away
and settle in a land
where no one breathes.

I had no idea how the downy puffs
of dandelions would be considered endangered
or how I would be told to hold my breath
as the doctor plucked another white tuff
from the torn stitches of the sky, and I had no idea
how even the wind would be condemned
to keep its mouth shut.

Who gave you the name

Who gave you the name
forgotten cradle,

who let the waters
from a thighs snuffed flame,

run down by the wheels,
big in the earth and
God in his Heaven

behind the pure stores
indescribable
pain of un-born voice,
who told you to fill
then left you alone.

Who calls you angel
by intervention
of your pharmacy,

who sent the word yes,
murmured by its trade:
always, by only
who see a birth fold
indescribably.

Who sent you that gift
you would not open,

who left you with eyes
numbered with handles,

who let you go out
and title the blue

believing perfumes
have unknown meanings

so someone out there
can go to a death.
And so, remember,

who leaves you to sleep,
who steals by your hand,
who lives in its room,
who burns with your name.

As the long awaited kiss

As the long awaited kiss
let its drum with dry
hammers against Campanula,
smelling as a nest of hearts,
happy as a silent bell
in a silent tower
peeling away its horse of blood
in the ringing pulse of lips,
the secret in the deaf bone,
the gentle thorn of seconds
reeling from pricks of blossoms,
your turning led to circles.

You called them eyes of Mary
for the blind disaster
went tapping its Sabbath
tapping, goodbye, goodbye,
goodbye for the day of gallows
is numbered in the heels of lovers
in the idol's fruit, the trapped crush
of Heaven's belly of cargos.

Tell them that you never knew, as a child
never knew, the scent of
contact…
Soon, they might say,
very soon.

Tell them but you've fallen in love
with doorways that never see
sunsets…
Soon, they might say.
Soon enough.

All your mourning mothers who
feel the screws of your loving,
loving the idea of loving,
will open their laps of cut flowers
and you will hear as they have seen
until they have tongued
the blind horse of blood
from their young needles…
Flowers, you might say,
Flowers.
Even though they
ring for the dead minute
in a place you cannot hear.

I see the huddled waters

I see the huddled waters
in the windy tides' compass.
I know of the wounded rain.

Her voice from a secret womb
made my leaves turn upside down
and let my fields surrender.

When her cloud broke with language
the fields hushed as if to fear
that moments' invitation.

My palms felt her cloudy breath
and my ravaged thighs yielded
in her invisible cult.

*   *   *

She leaves me as a lover—
A tree full of birds trembling.
Startled from fugitive beds.

Her pale figure of retreat
once again has calm waters
leaving me hushed in ruin.

I know of the wounded rain
that drapes on a pale shoulder:
A holy crisis falling.

As she fled she never turned.
She left me huddled waters
and I knew she would find me.

What *I* gave I shouldn't know.
I would not dishonor her.
She understands when I'm still.

Spook of huddled holes

appearing human after midnight.
You spook the sheep's clothing
right off my bones something angelic
I thought was nibbling
at the bait of my own body
                    Mr. shadow
who couldn't find his ass
from a hole in the ground.
I found that he could not not
wake up, but the dream, not.

The snow was ridiculous.
One could still see its fangs
as it went about the clouds of a child.

Not a spook of sun disturbed the dark,
mostly, that said my hands, mostly
can either search
down the throat
of what untimely swallowed
or choose to come out with.

The return of the Ram and the Month of Anvils

Carl laid his wrist down for a dream
and the still life of a lung
that moved the air from the frontiers
of his throat trying to unchain
the invisible ghost of his lips.
History was his slave for he believed in himself.
A hundred years later I went to find him
still dead with his guitar
and his lonely winter in Abraham's hat.
Rushing into his skull I couldn't help myself.
I wanted to be kissed
but there was no one to talk to.

A leviathan of hogs must have cleaned his bones
trying to prove just who can butcher who.
Only to be startled into a whisper…
I can still hear their galloping in the distance,
smothering the corners of his prairie I'm sure
with the flood of their mute scorched highways.
It must have been the red hoard or the mob
that suffered such a terrible loss of revenge
gathered inside the hollow of your tambourine.
Surprised by the scent of my orange blossoms
your sad angel spoke, *Let that old goat be lead again.*
This doesn't bode well for the fishes—

Eleven whispers of a dream are still unseen.
It is not in me to care for those animals.

As my childish angels speed a blade to fall on,
I cannot hunt from a womb of jasmine.
As I am but a quack with the glyph of flim-flam,
I enjoy my damage with red meat, oats, and figs.
In a grove of sycamores I began to give
and my joints began to ache for their limbs.
The enemy of laughter thundered through their songs.
Till the bonds of their youth became stillborn seasons.
What a suicide of sudden friendships!
Drunk, they cut their throats for the wine of blabber.

Soon I will gift your pickled lungs with my abortion.
My impatient love must seem some sort of a beast.
Truly my words are wings that either fly or fall
for all I know my beauty will go unlearned.
I have lived a long time waiting for the future.
Still, I blow you a cleft kiss from my virgin prints.
And so I have pled to my stubborn angel:
Whose child opens umbrellas of empty wombs
with a break-neck laughter of an anvil?
Should I fall from the sky with unknown madness?
Should my skylarks' tune be a whimsical hell?
Should I not follow?

Raphael kept watch over his hidden dumb star
until the idiot earth groaned for a hero.
And so it happened that I became a question
for ages, and to each, a poem for the hogs.
For nobody hears the sad rowing of a babe
until the echoes wave by their guilt.
Once I saw the fashionable scalps of slaves,
I found myself a broad city of danger.
I could have rushed into the traffic of still hearts

(I have so many histories to write with my blood.)
Yet, it isn't in me to care and so I can say
it's useless to torture the ghosts of pioneers.

Loosed by the hammer of holy beds I behave.
Rocking away into my cloven hemisphere.
Listen to the homeless song of my enemies
trying to unstop their throats through nails of time.
The dead have not forgotten my hour of fear
when the incision of my horn returns.
Somewhere in the crumpled black bell a little fire
dances on the edges of a strange new blade.
This is my gift—now my angel is your angel.
May the dreaming anatomies of your riots
gouge a still lung form a flower's torso.
Release your Ram with the laughter of an anvil!

The Calling Card

When I grow up I want to be a coin
tossed in a wishing well,
    a crossing guard for the blind.

I want to be a dream come true,
    a man who can't remember how it all began
    yet feels chased by someone he can't see.

When I grow up I want to breathe
one breath that doesn't remind me of another,
    a band that only knows how to play
    the wedding march
    when a bride is abandoned at the altar,
    at a wake after a deep dive in shallow water.

I want to arrive uninvited in this world.
I want to be a star.
I want to make it all the way
    back to where I was born
    and turn red.

I have a memory of a boy
blundering into a body of water,
    the prone position of a stone
    skipping across the waves.

I counted five birds
startled out of one tree,
or was it the other way around?

I know it means I was chosen
to be a man who stands
        behind a man
                and whispers in his ear,
to introduce myself as a fellow tailor
of small catastrophes
        waiting for winter to fashion something
        upon which I can hang my hat.

When I grow up I will walk up a stream
ensuring all fishes make it home,
        that there are no bones
        to get stuck in my throat.

The Last False Prophet

Having to tell him the world hadn't ended
the way he said it would
brought tears to our eyes.
Demons he cast out of the farmer's daughter
had raised families of their own.

The lepers he cured adorned their bodies
with tattoos of naked mermaids and anchors
and hung out on street corners
amounting to nothing alluring, tragic, or forlorn.

And so it went in the city
that had forsaken all manner of alchemy.
Metropolitan as it was,
they spoke the many languages of love and war.
Each had their name on a bullet
they were ready to take
for whomever got in their way.

On the day promised time
would shake the moths from our shadows
and we would see there was nothing left
to nibble away,
we found that we were still rooted
by a profound darkness.

Not knowing if he as a painter of picturesque lampposts
or a spider spinning its webs beneath its hues

we went sobbing door to door
until we found him preaching to a dog with three fleas.

At the very sight of us
he tore off his animal skins
and ran off laughing into a wilderness
of suicides dressed in sheep's clothing.
And we stood there in the awkward silence of that rapture
and could think of nothing better to do than return to Heaven.

The Anonymous Bone

I

The root of the spire bends to the soil

Deep in that bone where one and one
meet each other nameless
    like moonblind babes among the fiddleheads,
    sprays of virgin philters,
where sleeping armies flank the
charms of blank surrender
    like heroes spilling lonesome enclaves
    upon the thimbleberry's nimbus,
where petals spoke the pale skin
void of clabber,

how came there such a thunderclap?

Casting all the angels from my hip,
sent them scattering pitiful and lame
quivering on the rock bound bed,
half naked vitals down my leg,
    reeling like wolves, the primitive pack
let loose the dark spirit from my tree.

Staggering from the wood I was
unable to distinguish vein from vision.
The heaving retch in a faun's guise
    drew me in even closer,
driving ghosts mad upon my bone.
A savage chase that left me
              waking.

II

The kindred end that left a foul flame to hang loyalty

This reckless abundance, unyielding
        upon my green limb.
This barren heath, swinging
        upon my tortured bough
secured a grave mass,
a lifeless wide eyed Abel
twisted from the thrust of blood.

I was robbed from that manger.

As if by a brother's hand, I was
knocked from mercy's seat
to the strange dust.

"This is what brothers do"

And this, thrown from the pulp
to send crashing echoes to my stone
wave after wave of whispers to
tickle my insides sick,
poisoning thatch and loam,
snapping kindred timbers to feed
the foul flames of the
incestuous ingle,
driving black swifts aimless,

blinded by the smoke bled oven
void of loyalty's compass.

Not a single star shed its beams
    to guide eyes
or keep my country's faithful boarders.

So there, at the edge of a clearing,
I was left to lies

unwrapped to bear the rough cuts
    of rank fidelity.

This is what brothers do.
Oh, this is what brothers do!

III

Where all of Hell's arrows joyously cleave

To hunger, to feel that terrible teething
of hunger
lifting its head from the mangy bloom,
crippling stigmas and hounding the
battered mute petals
lusting for the hunt that makes them drip,
taking arrows through the milky thigh

where the tools of calamity skillfully corrupt
and put away the perennial boot hill.

So, then, digging the splendid speck of sap
I kiss the closed-lipped saint
and grasp the gales of her wanton itch.

Now see the innominate marrow
        yawning its dwarf vein,
bursting breech through the
        uncelebrated intestine.
Now see the heaving megacosm
        in the needle of the by-blow,
gleefully flailing its blunt pikes
        to languish on the ashen node

licking the absolute void of strident plentitude,
taking the arrows through the orphan blood

where the prayers of rampage hem
the heaven-wide whim.

So, then, plucking the fantastic florid flame
I lip the gods-head fronds
and burn with wicked out-stretched
lust for the throws of their frail aim.

Now see the wayward spire
    riding the pale skins' thermals
consuming clusters, suffering streams,
    of absent angels.
Now see the anonymous bone
    bleached of the boughs burden,
cleaving the stock of gallows
    and the hell-fired henchmen

raving, raving, raving in the razed tribe,
taking all the arrows through the Godly
                hip.

Your Name?

Are you now
or have you ever been
a scratch on the asylum wall
from a silver spoon?

A chain
between a convict's legs,
or between the watch
and the hand
of a hypnotist?

With all your T's crossed
and your I's dawning halos,

there's just enough religion
in you
to inspire doubt.

Of surgeon's thread.
Of butcher's twine.

From what, exactly,
that humming bird,
way out on a limb,
has built a nest

no bigger than a leaf
shuddering in the wind.

It goes without saying.

I made a mistake
when we first met.
Every attempt to erase it
left me only clipped,
dirty finger nails
from digging in the earth.

Now I know
where your associates
the exclamation
and question mark have gone,

why there is only an asterisk,
the whorl of its invisible wings
hovering over the lips,
a finger pointing
to a blank page.